D0049053

I Thee Wed

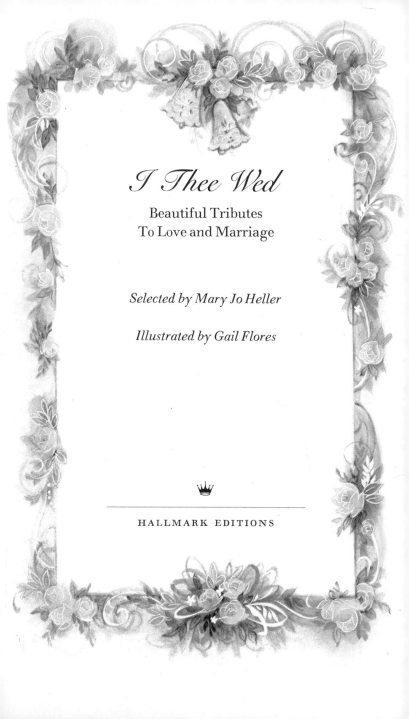

I Thee Wed

Beautiful Tributes
To Love and Marriage

Selected by Mary Jo Heller

Illustrated by Gail Flores

HALLMARK EDITIONS

I Thee Wed

To Have and To Hold

To have and to hold from this day forward, for better, for worse, for richer, for poorer, in sickness, and in health, to love and to cherish, till death do us part.

Book of Common Prayer, 1662

Joined for Life

What greater thing is there for two human souls than to feel that they are joined for life—to strengthen each other in all labor, to rest on each other in all sorrow, to minister to each other in all pain, to be one with each other in silent, unspeakable memories at the moment of the last parting.

George Eliot

How Do I Love Thee?
SONNET XLIII

How do I love thee? Let me count the ways.
I love thee to the depth and breadth and height
My soul can reach, when feeling out of sight
For the ends of Being and ideal Grace.
I love thee to the level of every day's
Most quiet need, by sun and candle-light.
I love thee freely, as men strive for Right;
I love thee purely, as they turn from Praise.
I love thee with the passion put to use
In my old griefs, and with my childhood's faith.
I love thee with a love I seemed to lose
With my lost saints,—I love thee with the breath,
Smiles, tears, of all my life!—and, if God choose,
I shall but love thee better after death.

Elizabeth Barrett Browning

A Wedding Tradition

Something Old . . .
Wear something old, from a bygone year
Which, like your love, is lasting and dear.

Something New . . .
Wear something new as a token, too,
Of the wonderful life that's beginning for you.

Something Borrowed . . .
Wear something borrowed and it will tell
That friends and loved ones wish you well.

Something Blue . . .
Wear something blue, like the skies above
When two hearts enter a world of love.

And a Penny, Too . . .
And place a penny inside your shoe
To assure good fortune your whole lives through.

Barbara Burrow

Prayer for a Bride

She is so beautiful, so pure, dear God.
    He is so tall, so fearless as they stand
Together at the threshold of their dreams.
    Oh, grant them length of days within the land.

Oh, always may her shining eyes be proud
    Of him to whom she plights her troth today.
And may he be as tender through the years—
    Theirs be a love time cannot take away!

Teach them our Father, marriage is much more
    Than one low-roofed, small house
        where two shall live.
More than new rooms resplendent with bright gifts
    Which happy friends, well-wishing them,
        may give.

Love bears all things, believeth, hopes, endures
    With stronger bonds than vows or nuptial kiss,
Love vaunteth not itself, seeks not its own,
    Love never faileth . . . Father, teach them this!
                                        Helen Welshimer

From 'The Bells'

Hear the mellow wedding bells,—Golden bells!
What a world of happiness their harmony foretells!
Through the balmy air of night
How they ring out their delight!
From the molten golden notes,
What a liquid ditty floats
To the turtle-dove that listens,
   while she gloats on the moon!
Oh, from out the sounding cells,
What a gush of euphony voluminously wells!
   How it swells!
     How it dwells
On the Future! How it tells
Of the rapture that impels
To the swinging and the ringing
Of the bells, bells, bells,
Of the bells, bells, bells, bells,
   Bells, bells, bells,—
To the rhyming and the chiming of the bells!

                      Edgar Allan Poe

To Be Womanly

To be womanly is to be loving. To be happy is to be given the opportunity to express that love. To be blessed is to have love returned. Love is not what you think. It does what mind cannot do, it goes where mind cannot follow. Its nature is transcendental and when we love we at once transcend ourselves and are most ourselves. This is the way man conceives God, and woman feels that in truly loving she is nearest heaven.

Jessamyn West

The True Measure

This is the true measure of love, when we believe that we alone can love, that no one could ever have loved so before us, and that no one will ever love in the same way after us.

Johann Wolfgang von Goethe

How Many Times Do I Love Thee?

How many times do I love thee, dear?
Tell me how many thoughts there be
   In the atmosphere
    Of a new-fall'n year,
Whose white and sable hours appear
The latest flake of Eternity:—
So many times do I love thee, dear.

How many times do I love again?
Tell me how many beads there are
   In a silver chain
    Of evening rain,
Unravelled from the tumbling main
And threading the eye of a yellow star:
So many times do I love again.

                  Thomas Lovell Beddoes

Let Me Not To The Marriage Of True Minds
SONNET CXVI

Let me not to the marriage of true minds
Admit impediments. Love is not love
Which alters when it alteration finds,
Or bends with the remover to remove:
O, no! it is an ever-fixed mark,
That looks on tempests and is never shaken;
It is the star to every wand'ring bark,
Whose worth's unknown, although his height
   be taken.
Love's not Time's fool, though rosy lips and cheeks
Within his bending sickle's compass come;
Love alters not with his brief hours and weeks,
But bears it out even to the edge of doom:—
     If this be error and upon me proved,
     I never writ, nor no man ever loved.
             William Shakespeare

The Voice Of My Beloved

The voice of my beloved! behold, he cometh leaping upon the mountains, skipping upon the hills.

My beloved is like a roe or a young hart: behold, he standeth behind our wall, he looketh forth at the windows, shewing himself through the lattice.

My beloved spake, and said unto me, Rise up, my love, my fair one, and come away.

For, lo, the winter is past, the rain is over and gone;

The flowers appear on the earth; the time of singing of birds is come, and the voice of the turtle is heard in our land;

The fig tree putteth forth her green figs, and the vines with the tender grape give a good smell. Arise, my love, my fair one, and come away.

Song of Solomon 2:8-13

The Night Before Marriage

Tomorrow, when I come to you,
   I put within your hand
Body and heart and soul, as who
   but women understand?

My lover, make me wholly yours
   in all the ways there are,
So a sweet bondage more endures
   than either lock or bar;

So that I never leave your breast
   to dream of other things,
But find in you my end-of-quest,
   my comfort . . . and my wings.

                Florence Jacobs

Communion

Of what avail are any words to tell
The glowing beauty of my thoughts of you?
It matters not I know the thoughts so well,
The faintest beauty will not glimmer through
The choicest words I write, the sweetest speech.
Silence were better: just a look or touch
Will tell you more, and bring us nearer each
To each than any spoken word, and much
More swiftly; for when silence wraps us round,
We see and feel the beauty that no word
Can paint, and tell our visions without sound,
In lovely tones no ear has ever heard,
Our silences are full of speech, and yet,
I know there is communion higher still,
And far beyond the bounds we mortals set,
For us to win, could we but love until
We reach that paradisal state which knows
No need of speech, or any human sign
To pierce the sense, and find what beauty glows
In each, and makes us, even now, divine.

T. Turner

Shall I Compare Thee To A Summer's Day?
SONNETT XVIII

Shall I compare thee to a summer's day?
Thou art more lovely and more temperate.
Rough winds do shake the darling buds of May,
And summer's lease hath all too short a date:
Sometime too hot the eye of heaven shines,
And often is his gold complexion dimmed;
And every fair from fair sometime declines,
By chance or nature's changing course untrimmed;
But thy eternal summer shall not fade,
Nor lose possession of that fair thou owest;
Nor shall Death brag thou wander'st in his shade,
When in eternal lines to time thou grow'st.

   So long as men can breathe, or eyes can see,
   So long lives this, and this gives life to thee.

William Shakespeare

Love Is a Constant Thing

There is no variableness, there is no turning,
When Love sets out upon its long highroad,
Storms cannot bind it, nor the hills deter it;
These cannot keep it from its own abode.
Lustily it climbs the hills of morning;
Lustily it strides the valley loam.
Its feet are swift upon the slopes of evening
Taking its sure way home.

There is no variableness, there is no turning;
The song upon its lips remains the same,
Years cannot stifle it, nor the dust smother
The song, if love be worthy of the name.
Life cannot blind its eyes at all, nor dying
Blot out its poignant, clear remembering;
Love is a permanent, a bright insistence,
Love is a constant thing.

Grace Noll Crowell

My Love Comes Walking

My love comes walking,
And these flowers
That never saw her 'til this day
Look up; but then
Bend down straightway.

My love sees nothing here but me,
Who never trembled thus before;
And glances down
Lest I do more.

My love is laughing;
Those wild things
Were never tame until I too,
Down-dropping, kissed
Her silvery shoe.

Mark Van Doren

Wedding Prayer

~~O Father, our hearts~~ are filled with great happi-
~~ness. This is our wedding day~~. We come before
you at the altar of love, pledging our lives and our
hearts to one another.

Grant that we may be ever true and loving, living together in such a way as to never bring shame
or heartbreak into our marriage. Temper our
hearts with kindness and understanding and rid
them of all pretense or jealousy.

Help us to be sweetheart, helpmate, friend and
guide, and together, may we meet the cares and
problems of life more bravely. And as time takes
away our youthful charm, may we find content-
ment in the greater joy of rich companionship.

May our home truly be a place of love and harmony where your Spirit is ever present,
~~Bless our wedding day, we pray, a~~nd walk beside us, Father, through all our life together.

Amen

The Greatest of These

Though I speak with the tongues of men and of angels, but have not love, I am become as sounding brass, or a tinkling cymbal. And though I have the gift of prophecy, and understand all mysteries, and all knowledge; and though I have all faith, so that I could move mountains, and have not love, I am nothing. And though I bestow all my goods to feed the poor and though I give my body to be burned, but have not love, it profiteth me nothing.

Love suffereth long, and is kind; love envieth not; doth not behave itself unseemly, seeketh not its own, is not easily provoked, thinketh no evil; rejoiceth not in iniquity, but rejoiceth in the truth; beareth all things, believeth all things, hopeth all things, endureth all things.

Love never faileth; but whether there be prophecies, they shall fail, whether there be tongues, they shall cease; whether there be knowledge, it shall vanish away. For we know in part, and we prophesy in part: but when that which is perfect is come, then that which is in part shall be done away. When I was a child, I spake as a child, I felt as a child, I thought as a child: but when I became a man, I put away childish things. For now we see in a glass, darkly; but then face to face; now I know in part; but then shall I know even as also I am known.

And now abideth faith, hope, love, these three; and the greatest of these is love.

I Corinthians 13

What Is Love?

To love very much is to love inadequately; we love —that is all. Love cannot be modified without being nullified. Love is a short word but it contains everything. Love means the body, the soul, the life, the entire being. We feel love as we feel the warmth of our blood, we breathe love as we breathe the air, we hold it in ourselves as we hold our thoughts. Nothing more exists for us. Love is not a word; it is a wordless state indicated by four letters.

Guy de Maupassant

Words of Love

To love means to decide independently to live with an equal partner, and to subordinate oneself to the formation of a new subject, a "we."

Fritz Kunkel

Love has the power to give in a moment what toil can scarcely reach in an age.

Goethe

Let your task be to render yourself worthy of love and this even more for your own happiness than for that of another.

Maurice Maeterlinck

Love is friendship set to music.   Pollock

An eternal hunger for love and beauty is my desire; I know now that those who possess bounty alone are naught but miserable, but to my spirit the sighs of lovers are more soothing than music of the lyre.

Kahlil Gibran

Marriage is a fusion of two hearts—the union of
two lives—the coming together of two tributaries,
which after being joined in marriage, will flow in
the same channel in the same direction . . . carry-
ing the same burdens of responsibility and obliga-
tion.

Peter Marshall

Let there be spaces in your togetherness.

Kahlil Gibran

This is the miracle that happens every time to
those who really love: the more they give, the
more they possess of that precious nourishing
love from which flowers and children have their
strength and which could help all human beings
if they would take it without doubting.

Rainer Maria Rilke

God, the best maker of all marriages,
Combine your hearts in one.

Shakespeare, *Henry V*

Love does not consist in gazing at each other but in looking outward together in the same direction.

Antoine de Saint-Exupery

Love is the enchanted dawn of every heart.

Lamartine

A man who has work that suits him and a wife he loves has squared his accounts with life.

Hegel

It is the man and woman united that makes the complete human being. Separate she lacks his force of body and strength of reason; he her softness, sensibility and acute discernment. Together they are most likely to succeed in the world.

Benjamin Franklin

Whatever woman may cast her lot with mine, should any ever do so, it is my intention to do all in my power to make her happy and contented; and there is nothing I can imagine that would make me more unhappy than to fail in the effort.

Abraham Lincoln

A good marriage is that in which each appoints the other guardian of his solitude.

Rainer Maria Rilke

Who can doubt that we exist only to love? Disguise it, in fact, as we will, we love without intermission. Where we seem most effectually to shut out love, it lies covert and concealed: we live not a moment exempt from its influence.

Blaise Pascal

It is by loving and not by being loved that one can come nearest the soul of another; yea, where two love it is the loving of each other, and not the being loved by each other, that originates and perfects and ensures their blessedness.

George MacDonald

It is difficult to define love. But we may say that in the soul, it is a ruling passion; in the mind, it is a close sympathy and affinity; in the body, a wholly secret and delicate longing to possess what we love —and this after much mystery.

La Rochefoucauld

The Newly-Wedded

Now the rite is duly done,
Now the word is spoken,
And the spell has made us one
Which may ne'er be broken;
Rest we, dearest, in our home,
Roam we o'er the heather:
We shall rest, and we shall roam,
Shall we not? together.

From this hour the summer rose
Sweeter breathes to charm us;
From this hour the winter snows
Lighter fall to harm us:
Fair or foul—on land or sea—
Come the wind or weather,
Best and worst, whate'er they be,
We shall share together . . . .

      Winthrop Mackworth Praed

The Legend of the Orange Blossoms

When the conquering Roman legions entered Portugal in the 3rd century, a marriage was arranged between the victorious Roman General and a beautiful princess of the Portuguese royal family. He had loved her ever since he first heard stories of her beauty and charm. Although she admired him, the princess also feared him because of the stories she had heard of his fierceness in battle.

At a sumptuous banquet before the wedding, the bride and groom saw one another for the first time. But silence came between them—a silence of awe on her part and a silence of love on his. After the banquet, the General walked alone across the Palace grounds to his encampment.

"How beautiful she is," he thought. "If only I could drive the fear from her eyes and let her know that I would love her tenderly all our lives."

As he walked, he found himself in a garden of small orange trees. "How fragrant they are! Like the perfume in her hair. And purest white, like her own pure soul."

Prompted by these thoughts, he gathered a spray of the lovely orange blossoms and sent them by messenger to the Princess. She was so touched by this tender gift from the great soldier that she shyly joined him in the garden. Soon they were walking hand in hand among the orange blossoms, and in her heart a quiet love grew that matched his own.

On their wedding day the Princess carried a spray of orange blossoms. Since that time these white flowers, a symbol of deepest love, have been carried by brides everywhere.

A Blessed Man

Blessed is the man that hath a virtuous wife, for the number of his days shall be double. A virtuous woman rejoiceth her husband, and he shall fulfill the years of his life in peace.

Ecclesiastes

The Bride

As slim and straight as the candles at her side
She stands, a flower with a flower's own grace.
Sheathed in the petaled satin of a bride,
Wrapped in a shimmering mist of fragile lace,
Serious and shy and very sweet,
She waits her lover's coming, eyes abrim
With happy dreams that are not yet complete
And only can be realized through him.

Here on the threshold of the years she stands,
So soon to leave her girlhood in the past.
God give her lover tender heart and hands
That the white radiance in her eyes may last;
God give her wisdom that she, too, may hold
His love till all the fires of earth grow cold.

                                    Grace Noll Crowell

The Bridesmaid

O bridesmaid, ere the happy knot was tied,
Thine eyes so wept that they could hardly see;
Thy sister smiled and said, "No tears for me!
A happy bridesmaid makes a happy bride."
And then, the couple standing side by side,
Love lighted down between them full of glee,
And over his left shoulder laugh'd at thee,
"O happy bridesmaid, make a happy bride."
And all at once a pleasant truth I learned,
For while the tender service made thee weep,
I loved thee for the tear thou couldst not hide,
And prest thy hand and knew the press returned,
And thought, "My life is sick of single sleep:
O happy bridesmaid, make a happy bride."

                              Alfred, Lord Tennyson

Whither Thou Goest . . .

And Ruth said: 'Entreat me not to leave thee, and
to return from following after thee; for whither
thou goest, I will go; and where thou lodgest, I will
lodge; thy people shall be my people, and thy God
my God; where thou diest, will I die, and there
will I be buried; the Lord do so to me, and more
also, if aught but death part thee and me.'

Ruth 1:16-17

A Prudent Wife

A prudent wife is from the Lord. The heart of her
husband doth safely trust her; she will do him
good, and not evil, all the days of her life. She
openeth her mouth with wisdom, and in her
tongue is the law of kindness. She looketh well to
the ways of her household, and eateth not the
bread of idleness. Her children arise and call her
blessed; her husband also, and he praiseth her.

Proverbs 31

Song To Celia

Drink to me only with thine eyes,
  And I will pledge with mine;
Or leave a kiss but in the cup,
  And I'll not look for wine.
The thirst that from the soul doth rise
  Doth ask a drink divine;
But might I of Jove's nectar sup,
  I would not change for thine.

I sent thee late a rosy wreath,
  Not so much honoring thee
As giving it a hope that there
  It could not withered be.
But thou thereon didst only breathe
  And sent'st it back to me;
Since when it grows, and smells, I swear,
  Not of itself but thee.

                                Ben Jonson

A Happy Marriage

You may have noticed that the Declaration of Independence does not number happiness, but rather the *pursuit* of it, among your inalienable rights. Happiness, like opportunity, knocks at doors but it doesn't break them down.... Thought and effort are required. It's not until you're engaged in it that you discover that the pursuit of happiness, this side of heaven, is really happiness itself.

Thus a happy marriage is based not so much on love as on the pursuit of love—the unremitting effort to develop your own love and to deserve your partner's. And as with happiness, so the pursuit of love becomes love itself.

Virginia and Louis Baldwin

Oblation

Oh, how my body blooms from every vein,
more fragrant, since you came into my ken.
See how I walk, more slender and upright,
and you wait calmly—and who are you, then?

Behold: I feel that I have left me far
behind and shed my old life, leaf by leaf,
till finally there is nothing but the star
of your smile shining richly on our life.

Everything that through my childhood years
was nameless still and glistening like water
I will christen after you before the altar,
which is made radiant by your shining hair,
the altar which your breasts have lightly crowned.

Rainer Maria Rilke
(Tr.C. F. MacIntyre)

True Love
From LOVE

True Love is but a humble, low-born thing,
And hath its food served up in earthen ware;
It is a thing to walk with, hand in hand,
Through the everydayness of this work-day world,
Baring its tender feet to every flint,
Yet letting not one heart-beat go astray
From Beauty's law of plainness and content;
A simple, fireside thing, whose quiet smile
Can warm earth's poorest hovel to a home . . . .
Such is true Love, which steals into the heart
With feet as silent as the lightsome dawn
That kisses smooth the rough brows of the dark,
And hath its will through blissful gentleness,
Not like a rocket, which, with passionate glare,
Whirs suddenly up, then bursts, and leaves
   the night
Painfully quivering on the dazed eyes;
A love that gives and takes, that seeth faults,
Not with flaw-seeking eyes like needle points,
But loving-kindly ever looks them down

With the o'ercoming faith that still forgives;
A love that shall be new and fresh each hour,
As is the sunset's golden mystery
Or the sweet coming of the evening-star,
Alike, and yet most unlike, every day,
And seeming ever best and fairest now . . . .

James Russell Lowell

Unceasing Love

It is in the nature of that love which deserves the
name not to cease. We love that which is lovable.
That which is most lovable is the secret beauty in
another's nature. Love is the feeling evoked by an-
ticipation of union with that beauty. It constantly
recreates itself and is intensified even while
thwarted. It is a longing anticipating its satisfac-
tion; it is the constant unwillingness to be separated from the object of its quest.

Felix Adler

For Those Who Love

Time is . . .
Too slow for those who wait,
Too swift for those who fear,
Too long for those who grieve,
Too short for those who rejoice;
But for those who love, time is eternity.

Henry Van Dyke

I Have No Life But This

I have no life but this—
To lead it here—
Nor any death but lest
Dispelled from there—

Nor tie to earths to come—
Nor action new—
Except through this extent—
The realm of you.

Emily Dickinson

The Basic Passion

Love is the basic passion of man. Every emotion of the heart is reducible to it. Without love we would never become better, for love is the impetus to perfection, the fulfillment of what we have not . . . .

Love is an inclination or a tendency to seek what seems good. The lover seeks union with the good which is loved in order to be perfected by it. The mystery of all love is that it actually precedes every act of choice; one chooses because he loves, he does not love because he chooses. As St. Thomas put it, "All other passions and appetites presuppose love as their first root."

Fulton J. Sheen

I Love You

I love you for what you are, but I love you yet more for what you are going to be.

I love you not so much for your realities as for your ideals. I pray for your desires that they may be great, rather than for your satisfactions, which may be so hazardously little.

A satisfied flower is one whose petals are about to fall. The most beautiful rose is one hardly more than a bud wherein the pangs and ecstasies of desire are working for larger and finer growth.

Not always shall you be what you are now.

You are going forward toward something great. I am on the way with you and therefore I love you.

Carl Sandburg

Reading (handwritten)

Married Love

Married living needs the continuance of the dash and sparkle of romantic love. But the relation of romantic love to married love is somewhat like that of a little tree to the larger tree which it later becomes. It has life and fresh young energy that enables it to grow. When it has grown into a larger tree its heart and vitality are still there but, with continued life, it has taken new rings of growth, its branches have spread wider and its roots have gone deeper. Moreover it bears flowers and fruit which the little tree did not produce.

Married love is love woven into a pattern of living. It has in it the elements of understanding and of the passionate kindness of husband and wife toward each other. It is rich in the many-sided joys of life because each is more concerned with giving joy than with grasping it for himself. And joys are most truly experienced when they are most fully shared.

Leland Foster Wood

Of Marriage

Here Love begins to render the prose of Life into hymns and canticles of praise, with music that is set by night, to be sung in the day. Here Love's longing draws back the veil, and illumines the recesses of the heart, creating a happiness that no other happiness can surpass but that of the Soul when she embraces God.

Marriage is the union of two divinities that a third might be born on earth. It is the union of two souls in a strong love for the abolishment of separateness. It is that higher unity which fuses the separate unities within the two spirits. It is the golden ring in a chain whose beginning is a glance, and whose ending is Eternity. It is the pure rain that falls from an unblemished sky to fructify and bless the fields of divine Nature.

As the first glance from the eyes of the beloved is like a seed sown in the human heart, and the first kiss of her lips like a flower upon the branch of the Tree of Life, so the union of two lovers in marriage is like the first fruit of the first flower of that seed.

Kahlil Gibran

'My True-Love Hath My Heart'

My true-love hath my heart, and I have his,
By just exchange one for the other given:
I hold his dear, and mine he cannot miss;
There never was a better bargain driven:
His heart in me keeps him and me in one,
My heart in him his thoughts and senses guides:
He loves my heart, for once it was his own,
I cherish his, because in me it bides.

His heart his wound received from my sight;
My heart was wounded from his wounded heart;
For as from me, on him his hurt did light,
So still me thought in me his heart did smart:
Both equal hurt, in this change sought our bliss:
My true love hath my heart, and I have his.

Philip Sidney

Love's Source

The marriage service leaves us looking out along a road that leads on to endless joy. There will be hardships along that road, and disappointments. To travel it will require strong disciplines and intelligently worked-out ways. Much that is ahead is uncertain, but some things can be depended on as absolutely sure. "Faith, hope, love abide, these three; but the greatest of these is love."

The bride and groom can set forth with high hearts because they have faith in each other which is founded on their faith in God. They can face the future full of hope because they know what will bring their marriage its daily comforts and ultimate success. Side by side they can start down across the years held to each other by a love whose source is in the heart of God.

George E. Sweazey

She Walks in Beauty

She walks in beauty like the night
Of cloudless climes and starry skies;
And all that's best of dark and bright
Meets in her aspect and her eyes:
Thus mellow'd to that tender light
Which heaven to gaudy day denies.

One shade the more, one ray the less,
Had half impair'd the nameless grace
Which waves in every raven tress,
Or softly lightens o'er her face—
Where thoughts serenely sweet express
How pure, how dear their dwelling-place.

And on that cheek, and o'er that brow,
So soft, so calm, yet eloquent,
The smiles that win, the tints that glow,
But tell of days in goodness spent,
A mind at peace with all below,
A heart whose love is innocent.

George Gordon, Lord Byron

The Law of Love

What the law of gravity is to stars and sun, the law of love is to men and women . . . . We all retain our sanity by the conviction that we are needed today and tomorrow, and by the memory of love that we have experienced—given or received— which already has become blood of our blood and spirit of our spirit.

Joshua Loth Liebman

Men Marry What They Need. I Marry You

Men marry what they need. I marry you,
morning by morning, day by day, night by night,
and every marriage makes this marriage new.

In the broken name of heaven, in the light
that shatters granite, by the spitting shore,
in air that leaps and wobbles like a kite,

I marry you from time and a great door
is shut and stays shut against wind, sea, stone,
sunburst, and heavenfall. And home once more

inside our walls of skin and struts of bone,
man-woman, woman-man, and each the other,
I marry you by all dark and all dawn

and learn to let time spend. Why should I bother
the flies about me? Let them buzz and do.
Men marry their queen, their daughter, or their
    mother

by names they prove, but that thin buzz whines
    through:
when reason falls to reasons, cause is true.
Men marry what they need. I marry you.

                                    John Ciardi

The Story of the Bridal Veil

When Abraham was far advanced in years he sent his most trusted servant to Mesopotamia to find a wife for his son, Isaac. With ten camels and many gifts—silver, gold, and raiment—the servant arrived at his destination. Tired and thirsty from his journey, he approached a well, where he saw a comely young woman. Her name was Rebecca.

As the servant came near, Rebecca covered her face with her veil, as was the custom among women of virtue. He asked her for water and she answered, "Drink, and I will give your camels drink also." These words were the sign that the servant had prayed to God for. They told him this was the woman who should be Isaac's wife.

The servant explained his mission to Rebecca, and she urged him to see Bethuel, her father. When Bethuel had heard the servant's words, he said it was the Lord's will that Rebecca go to Isaac. Gifts were given to the family, and Rebecca and the servant left on the journey back.

Issac was in the fields when Rebecca and the servant approached. Rebecca saw Isaac, and immediately alighted from her camel. She removed her veil, and went to Isaac, and he took her into his home. They became husband and wife.

Through history the bridal veil has been worn as Rebecca wore her veil. In the act of removing it, the bride tells her groom that she has given herself to him for life.

Based on The Book of Genesis

Never marry but for love, but see that thou lovest what is lovely.

William Penn

The aspiration of lovers: to be as necessary to each other as the World to God, and God to the World.

Richard Garnett

Circles

The sun is round,
A crown is round,
And so, indeed,
A perfect sound.
The earth is round,
The eye is round;
So the horizon's curve
Is found.
The moon is round,
A ring is round;
My love is in
A circle bound.

      Mary Christine Best

My Heart Has Its Love

The sea has its pearls,
The heaven its stars—
But my heart, my heart,
My heart has its love!

      Heinrich Heine

To His Love

An old silver church in a forest
Is my love for you.
The trees around it
Are words that I have stolen from your heart.
An old silver bell, the last smile you gave,
Hangs at the top of my church.
It rings only when you come through the forest
And stand beside it.
And then it has no need for ringing,
For your voice takes its place.

Maxwell Bodenheim

Love is a circle, that doth restless move
In the same sweet eternity of Love.

Robert Herrick

Unity

Heart of my heart, the world is young:
Love lies hidden in every rose,
Every song that the skylark sung
Once, we thought, must come to a close:
Now we know the spirit of song,
Song that is merged in the chant of the whole,
Hand in hand as we wander along,
What should we doubt of the years that roll?

Heart of my heart, we cannot die!
Love triumphant in flower and tree,
Every life that laughs at the sky
Tells us nothing can cease to be;
One, we are one with a song today,
One with the clover that scents the wold,
One with the Unknown, far away,
One with the stars, when earth grows old.

Heart of my heart, we are one with the wind,
One with the clouds that are whirled o'er the lea,
One in many O broken and blind,
One as the waves are at one with the sea!
Ay! when life seems scattered apart,
Darkens, ends as a tale that is told,
One, we are one, O heart of my heart,
One, still one, while the world grows old.

Alfred Noyes

Marriage resembles a pair of shears, so joined that they cannot be separated, often moving in opposite directions, yet always punishing anyone who comes between them.

Sydney Smith

A Man's Choice

Women have been immortalized in sonnets, made forever permanent in marble, and tinted magnificently in oils on canvas. But what is it that makes them beautiful and loved? It may be perfection of physical form; it may be the degree of sympathy, intelligence, and compassion they can express. It is certainly nice for a woman to have all these things, but this is not necessarily why they are beautiful and loved . . . . What really makes a woman beautiful and loved is—a man. The moment a man chooses her for his own, she automatically enters the hall of fame of the beautiful and the loved.

Harry Golden

For Every Bride

For every bride who walks with shining faith
Into the day new promise has begun;
I'd ask not castles reaching to the sun
Nor golden doors to smug security,
But only this . . .
May love have kept for her,
When twenty other years have come and gone,
The wonder of the rose and purple dawn,
The thrill in every bud that heralds spring,
The peace of evening lights in twilight skies,
The joy of rain upon the thirsty grass . . .
And dreams to challenge all the years that pass
To dim that star today lights in her eyes.

Dixie Willson

To My Dear And Loving Husband

If ever two were one, then surely we.
If ever man were lov'd by wife, then thee.
If ever wife was happy in a man,
Compare with me, ye women, if you can.
I prize thy love more than whole Mines of gold,
Or all the riches that the East doth hold.
My love is such that Rivers cannot quench,
Nor aught but love from thee give recompense.
Thy love is such I can no way repay;
The heavens reward thee manifold I pray.
Then while we live, in love let's so perservere,
That when we live no more, we may live ever.

Anne Bradstreet

Kind is my love today, tomorrow kind,
Still constant in a wondrous excellence.

Shakespeare

Marriage

Going my way of old
Contented more or less
I dreamt not life could hold
Such happiness.

I dreamt not that love's way
Could keep the golden height
Day after happy day,
Night after night.

      Wilfrid Wilson Gibson

Set at The Castle Press in Intertype Walbaum, a light,
open typeface designed by Justus Erich Walbaum
(1768-1839), a type founder at Goslar and at Weimar.
Printed on Hallmark Eggshell Book paper.
Designed by Virginia Orchard.